EMPATH 1

A COLLECTION OF POETRY WRITTEN

BY

MARC HATTER

DEDICATION

TO
NANNY DOT
CHARLOTTE HATTER
EMILY HATTER

ACKNOWLEDGMENTS

I would like to just mention a few people's names who along with my own life experiences, have inspired me to write what's written in this book.
Dorothy Davies
Claire Douglas
David Hatter
Cyrelle Zimmerman
Jason Hatter
Charlotte Hatter
Emily Hatter
Emma Sohar
Phillipa Freeman
Ronald Burn

A Life . . .

Life is hard,
life is not easy,
nothing in life is given to you freely.
Love is found,
and it's lost,
just as quickly,
and with a cost.
You can give so much without the blink of
an eye,
but with giving,
so people will lie.
Life pushes you this way,
and then that.
But what really matters is how you react.
Always stay strong,
and always be nice.
As with this life,
you can't live it twice.
You only have one,
so make sure it's right.
Or it will be lonely,
this thing,
your life.

A Woman On The Streets

The life of a women on the street is often
not very up beat.
As you never get in front of the hard life on
the street.
When you feel like you're on the road to
nowhere.
All you need to do is just start to care,
about your own personal welfare.
You see all those men they just don't care,
well they do but not about you,
as the way they see it is,
they pay you to be there.
There is no love there,
its only lust that's sold there.
You can make a life there,
but surely being on social or welfare,
would be a better life then
making money there.
So if you really care,
your stop yourself from being there.
Turn your life around,
make a fresh start somewhere,
anywhere but just not there.

See out there are people that really care.
So make that change get off the streets,
then your find your life will be more
complete.
Then your see that your street,
will become, more and more,
upbeat . . .

<u>Alone</u>

Alone I sit in my life right now,
but surrounded by family.
But alone I sit right now,
feel like how can this be.
However this life I lead,
with this loneliness I feed.
It doesn't come from me.
I've never asked to feel the way I feel right
now,
with this loneliness I deal.
Sad as it is, or is not,
the feeling is something maybe
we all forgot.
But to some it's real,
this loneliness that we can feel.
It doesn't turn and it doesn't leave,
it surrounds us,
it starts to feed.
So alone I sit in my life right now,
but surrounded by family.
Not everyone has that luxury,
that family surrounding thee.
So alone they feel,
no one to visit,
to help them heal.

The loneliness that surrounds them,
that wasn't their deal.
I'm all alone,
some people just can't believe,
that's where they've ended,
with now no family.
Alone I sit in my life right now,
as I'm no longer with family.
It's only now I truly understand,
how loneliness can breed.
With no warning with no sign,
life changes drastically,
for family that was once there,
have all gone and left me be.
So those that still have family,
should be grateful and full of glee.
But should take some time to understand,
that this way may not always be.

Sister

Cockney rhyming slang.
Skin and blister, Sister.
My Sister, I would so miss her.
If I didn't have my Sister,
god knows how much I'd miss her.
You see my Sister is that one,
the mother sister.
That sister that always knows how sort out
a Mr.
The kind of sister that will always give,
everything from within her.
I would give a kidney for my sister,
easy.
Cause none of us would wona miss her.
She's a solid sister,
a rock,
as she's always giving more than she's got.
She's the type of girl you always want
near ya.
As she always supports all those most dear
to her.
You see what she gives,
is way more than what we ever give to her.
So she needs to understand,
how much we love her.

Cause we only have one life,
to live with each other.
My sister,
I should tell you a lot more that I love ya,
and I'm always here for ya.
You're my one and only, SISTER.

Brother

Brother,
blessed with the blood from within each
other.
No other friendship can compare to that of
our brother.
But as brothers we need to spend time
apart, from one another.
You see,
to have the relationship we have,
is because we don't see a lot,
of each other.
But we've always known,
that we're there,
as we're brothers.
No matter how much we annoy one
another other.
You and I both know where to draw the
line,
from each other.
So I say this to you dear brother.
I'm always guna be your younger other.
So please take the time to always mutter,
words to your younger brother.
That I'll always love ya,
my BROTHER.

24 Hours

Ended day,

started night,

is one wrong,

is the other right.

Goodbye my day,

hello my night,

just another 24-hour sight.

Cousins

I got a cousin she is well all right,
she lives away,
way out a site.
Now I ain't just got one though,
I got number two,
and the other one, well,
she ain't the full screw.
But cousin number two,
she's like cousin number one,
put them both together,
and you got a whole lot a of fun.
Now these two diamond lasses,
you ain't never guna find,
in any nook or cranny,
in any kinda tyne.
Now they love me dearly,
as I do there mine.
The very finest cousins,
yor ever bloody find.
But I do know one thing with them,
that time is not an issue.
There always be there for me,
with hand heart and tissues.
My cousin's mean a lot to me,
and I very rarely tell them.

So here's a poem for you all,
to let you know how much,
your cousins from down south you know,
love you very much.

Daze

Like a movie and the hands of a clock,
we watch,
we look.
We are forever locked in that moment,
of that time,
that clock,
that movie.
Hoping it was reality,
forever thinking,
wishing,
that we could turn it on,
and off,
and be a part of what we see,
or what we watch.
But that's not reality,
it's not a movie,
or a clock,
we can't just turn it on and off.
This thing called life,
it's always none stop,
with no rewind,
without a pause, without a stop.
Are lives like a movie,
like that clock,
tick tock.

Helping others

I would like to feel a thousand thoughts,
And I would like to be anyone's course.
Some will rise and some will fall.
So reach out before the
judgement calls.
Help another in their time of fall.
Don't be shy step forward and tall.
Give what you can and don't be called,
don't be labelled and don't be fooled.
Just one difference can make it all,
a better place for the one that falls.
We are life we are one and all,
so how can two lives be so difficult.
How is one blessed and one is minimal.
We should all help each other,
To be equal.

<u>From The Dark To The Light</u>

In the dark of the dark we are left marked,
with scars.
Some run deep,
that we keep locked beneath.
Others are visible,
and to those close can be quite visual.
But it's how we deal with the dark pains we
feel.
And how those around us help to heal.
From loss to gain we move on from the
pain.
As we grow from each time and turn,
from within the darkness is where learn.
But from our battles we seem muster,
strengths and courage from within one
another.
We rise we fall, but always try to stand tall.
As I think there's a fighter within us all.
But some need help more than others,
to find that strength,
from within that darkness.
So together we gather,
we pull each other out,
of the darkness we reach out.
To be in the light,

we aspire to be,
each and every one of us,
sharing the happiness,
and are free.

Got To believe

It's like you can't believe your wrong,
and you don't believe your strong, enough,
for you and me,
you can't believe.
So I tell you that your wrong,
that your just as strong as me,
why don't you believe.
So stand up for yourself,
don't hesitate to show your wealth,
in how strong you are.
You see people see your weakness,
and will exploit it till your feetless,
and can't stand strong.
So show them your wealth,
show them your strength.
Once they feel your confidence,
they'll know they can't carry on with this,
the way it is.
So you see you have a choice with this,
stand up and make that noise be quick.
Life doesn't last that long,
make it so how you want it to carry on,
but be quick.
Once you've made the changes strong,
you won't feel so heavy your run along,

without those that coursed you wrong.
See now you believe how you are strong,
See,
I wasn't wrong.

How It Should Be

The life you lead should be free from
commotion.
You see all you need is to move the
emotion,
to be free.
That doesn't come easy to some in the
moment.
But one should take the time,
to rise from that one that has holds on
them.
It's not always easy to step forward and
show them.
To take control of your life and be
wholesome, again.
But the strength is within all,
everyone can find it with them.
That your life now has the power to
overcome from them.
You see your life is now free once again.
You can move forward and progress
without them.
Life will be full, and apart from them.
You see all you need is lead yourself

once again.
Then their see that your now in
control again.
Just stand tall,
stand proud and show them.
That once again,
that person doesn't control them.
You're now the one,
that stands,
over them.

I Need You To Know

I need you to know your what makes me
glow.
I need you to know I just can't let you go.
I need you to know it's worth the fight.
I need you to know things can be made
right.
I need you to know not to give up,
I need you to know you have to man up,
I need you to know enough is enough.
I need you to know I'll never give up.
I need you to know it's all on you,
but I need you to know I'm right here for
you.
I need you to know you've done this
before,
so this is not an unfamiliar door.
I need you to know your life will blossom.
But you need to know not to start
from the bottom.
I need you to know,
that all you need,
is to stand once again,
on you own two feet.

I Want You And You Want Me

I want you and you want me,
So how comes this thing between us is so
hard to be.
I am lost I'm frightened,
I need you to help give us guidance.
I know things aren't always easy,
but I do give you my love all and
completely.
I want to hug and to hold you tightly,
with all the love that I have inside me.
But I know I can't,
as you won't let me near.
So I'll give you the time and space you
need to adjust,
to make your thoughts clear and a
must.
I cannot call as our speech isn't easy,
so I'll put my words to you, to you dearly.
Love you so much that words cannot touch,
only my presents can do such a must.
My heart is yours and yours only,
so I hope you can see,
all I want,
is your love only.

I Wonna

I wonna feel your touch,
I wonna feel your skin.
I wonna feel your everything.
I wonna feel your love,
I wonna feel your heart.
I wonna feel the warmth of your breath
beside me until we part.
I wonna feel you getting better,
I wonna know you're on the mend.
But at this present moment in time, it's
hard to even be your friend.
I wonna life with you I really,
really do.
But you have to want me,
as much as I want you.
Without the worry that
I have if your or write or wrong.
But what I wonna feel from you,
is that you're getting yourself strong.
I wonna let you know right now that I don't
things are good.
So you need see the future,
as a clear head really should.
I wonna let you know right now,
that you need to search real deep.

But not only for yourself my love,
but for those nearly out of reach.
I wonna let you know my love,
with things the way are,
I think we're best as you say,
spending some time apart.
Not because I want that,
but because it's what you need.
To return yourself fully back,
to who you used to be.

Life Is Hard

Life is hard when you're having to learn
from not knowing which way to turn.
Life is hard having to stop this,
and start that,
not knowing what's the right track.
Life is hard as you have to make hard
choices,
listening to everyone's voices,
giving you all these positive and negative
choices.
Life is hard having all these emotions,
running around your mind causing blurred
commotion.
Life is hard there's no easy way out,
it's fight or flight without a doubt.
Life is hard when there's no one to guide
you,
no one to help,
as no one can decide for you.
Life is hard as every choice you make,
changes your walk-in life,
and determines the paths you take.
Life is hard so take time to listen,
take time to think,
make the right difference. . .

Love Train

I've missed you and you've missed me.
So you see this love is supposed to be.
We cannot hide it we cannot flee,
as together is where we are destined to
be.
Like a love train that we so rock.
It has no driver and there is no stop.
Without a driver and now where to hide.
This ever-growing love thing will guide.
Ever growing and never stopping,
is our love train that we so rock in.
It carries on it will not stop,
for our love will always rock.

Love

Love draws us together,
in lots of different ways.
We have lots of different feelings,
in each and every day.
For love is something we wish to feel,
and wish to give away.
But only to those dear to us,
will we open up this way.
Love is such a powerful thing,
such joy and happiness it brings.
But not everyone uses the love they bring,
for the good of the other,
that they're involved in.
For the power, the passion,
the strength of a reaction,
is something that some can't imagine.
Some can't hold,
some can't control,
that's why some shouldn't get involved.
As love should be so sacred,
love should be so true.
As whoever you're in love with,
should be the only one with you.

My Heart My World

There is no need for me to search,
no need for me to look.
As I have found the final chapter of
my book,
in you.
You are my sweetheart my one true love,
as we fit like hand and glove.
You make me whole,
you make me feel loved,
you make feel like I'm enough.
I am yours and you are mine,
now we both know the future will be fine. .
You are my love my one and only
 . . . my heart . . . my world

Nan

Ashes to ashes dust to dust,
is the usual words that we must.
But not today not for you,
some better words all but a few.
As no pill or potion can replace you,
or our feelings we have for you.
As you were the greatest,
you were God's best,
the best ever nanny,
that he's ever laid to rest.
You were our savour you were our rock,
our mother, our grandmother,
as you took care of your flock.
Now at this time,
you wouldn't want us to be sad.
But raise our thoughts cast back our
minds,
and remember the best and
most flavorous times.
As there never forgotten,
as there in our minds,
is those very special moments of kind.
Those ones when you were by are sides,
laughing and chatting,
those happy times.

But this is not the end for you and us,
but merely a brief goodbye till we meet the
dust.
So you see from us to you,
we'll all see you,
very,
very soon.

Remembering Nan

A year this time we said goodbyes.
To the one we held close our lives.
Up in the stars is where you've gone,
two worlds apart but not for long.
You can't be here you can't be there,
but we feel you everywhere.
Not in the flesh not in person,
but in our memories,
you're still that same person.
That special lady that helped us so much,
that in our memories you can still be
touched.
You're that special lady the only one,
that took the place of our mum.
So together now you both will be,
happy again as families should be.
Now we take this time to remember you
all,
as we send up these lanterns of love from
us all.

Reach

Where do you reach out to, who?
when you need to reach out,
who do you reach to?
who reaches out to you.
Can anyone know what you need,
once you've made that step and reached
out.
Can they really help,
are they equipped to help?
"I'm always here if you need me,
whatever."
A phrase people use to casualty,
but to others mean so much more.
Sometimes in life when we feel we need to
hear that phrase, that person.
They are not there, not the one.
Maybe all we need is to search deeper
within ourselves.
As within our own struggles,
we find,
that reach,
that phrase,
that person,
we find,
ourselves.

People

People.
It's funny how people can change are way
of thinking and feeling.
People.
Isn't it strange how a person can just lift
your day and your way of feeling.
People.
It's hard to imagine that a person would
give you such a smile just by being around.
People.
A hard and heavy day can and be uplifted,
just by a single message from that person.
People.
Can give and receive such happiness with a
small token,
a presence, call or emoji message.
People.
How one's life can be so intermittently
changed by just that one other person.
People.
That person exchanges a small piece of
life with every moment of every contact
that you share.

People.
Give so much and so freely without even
knowing what they have given.
People.
We should all make sure we are no stranger
to one another.
People.
As a person you should always be grateful,
for those other people.

Technology

Technology is here,
technology is there,
this evil stuff is everywhere.
Pinch me this, expand me that,
is this where are lives are at.
Take a picture here, take a picture there,
should we all at this point stop and share.
At someone's gain, at someone's loss,
this technology comes with such a cost.
Is it yours, or is it mine,
the technology of our time.
No, its not mine, nor yours,
but the whole world's floors of course.
It bares such sorry and such loss,
this ever-growing technology cost.
It can be good though in the right hands,
it can show the great and the good of the
lands.
But everyone in time has felt the cost,
of the good,
the bad,
of this future lost,
technology?

Time

Time is precious,
as life can be so short.
Time is something that doesn't pay a lot of
thought.
Time can move so swiftly,
when life can be so busy.
Time can be drawn out,
it can feel like ages without a bout.
Time isn't something that we should take
for granted.
As this time thing,
is quickly stopped and started.
That's how loved ones,
join us and are parted.
Time is never ending,
it's forever flowing,
never stopping,
as its forever showing.

That Time

My life has been so hard,
so hard right from the start.
Never knowing one day from another,
all that pain just seemed to muster,
I was so young.
I never new how to handle,
such emotion such scandal,
it tore me apart.
At the time I went inside,
and I just cried and I cried,
felt like I'd died.
It wasn't just me,
I wasn't alone,
was one of three,
all be it felt like,
just me.
And at that time at that moment,
something precious had be stolen,
how can this be.
Can't believe what's happened,
whole worlds shattered and abandoned,
you were gone.
So, I miss you.

Nothing can help the pain,
life will never be the same.
Ever again.
I miss you . . .

Up

Tragedy tests us,

all you have to do is wake Up.

Loss changes us,

all you have to do is strengthen Up.

Life shows us,

all you have to do is step Up.

What Is Hope

Hope.
What is hope.
Is hope that one thing that keeps us
moving.
Or is it something but like a dream,
doesn't seem reel.
Maybe it isn't real.
Hope,
is it a positive or a negative?
To be hopeful or hopefully about
something that may or may not be.
Should we be more or less hopeful.
As if what we hope for materialises
and does happen,
does that do more damage than if does
not?
So ask yourself,
what is hope?
Do you really need it?
does it really help us?
Or is it just another figment of societies
broadcasting?

Wishing You Were With Me

Sometimes when I'm looking out the
window,
I see your face gazing back at me.
Sometimes when I'm staring at the stars,
I see your face looking down at me.
And the days when I'm running out of
patience,
I feel your love surrounding me.
But I know for the rest of my life time,
you won't be sharing yours with me.
It's hard to explain or find reason,
that's why it's so difficult to be free.
As life doesn't show us the reasons,
You're not sharing yours with me.
So I find myself in a place,
Where I really don't want to be.
I want to be in a place,
where your still sharing life with me.

You And Me

You are you and I am me,
let's not question what may or may not be.
For the past is the past it cannot see,
the future that lays for you and me.
We both have floors we both have are
struggles,
but together maybe it won't feel doubled.
Kindness towards you, and towards me,
given time we might find the key.
The key to friendship the key to trust,
maybe given time the key to lust.
Time is all that we need in life,
to see if you and I are right.
We may come together,
if we are meant to be.
But if not,
friends we'll definitely be.

The Working Thing

The last thing we look forward to is work.
So a working life isn't easy,
a lot of people take it too freely.
But when you're out all hours providing for
yours dearly.
They should take some time to appreciate
your commitment to them,
deeply.
Now a working life isn't all dreary,
as once you've earnt it can help provide
strength and stability.
A working life,
a working wage,
can bring so much to your young coming of
age.
You see a wage can bring so much,
some pleasure,
for that person that earnt that crust.
They say that money makes the world go
round,
but it's not,
that gives off the wrong sound.
You see sleep and rest is a must at best,
where those workers lay their weary heads.

To recuperate,
to carry on,
of the evolution of this worlds song.
See money doesn't make the world go
round,
its these everyday people that get pushed
into the ground.
So enjoy what you have,
what a working life brings.
As life can be so hard constantly doing . . .
The working . . .
Thing . . .

Christmas

At this special time of year,
that brings so much love a cheer.
Let's not forget about the lonely ones,
the people that haven't got anyone.
No one's close to them this year,
giving to them what we hold dear.
The fun, laughter the togetherness,
that's what they wish for like the rest of us.
So take the time, take a moment,
and reflect on what hasn't be stolen.
The rest of this day and this season,
with our loved ones together with reason.
We have so much but it's never enough,
so think of those without such luck.
Grateful is what we should be,
as we have so much more,
then we really need?

Is It Worth It

So I need to know,
is it time to let my love for you go?
So I need to know,
can I move on,
on my own?
But then I feel like I'll forget you,
and our love will never been known.
So I ask you to show me,
is it worth me hanging on?
So I ask you to give me,
a sign that it's not wrong.
So I ask you for the last time,
is it worth fighting and carrying on.
You're the only one that can tell me?
is it off or is it on.
Or is it that our love,
has finally sung,
its last song.

Tired Eyes And Matchsticks

Children and tiredness go hand in hand,
the fatherly life we have is always trying,
and can never be planned.
The 4am mornings the 4pm snoozes,
us we're the ones that bare the tiredness
bruises.
But it's not a loss,
merely but a cost,
to us of how much we want to watch,
and sacrifice for our child's future not to be
a loss.
Which will be the greatest got,
when you see them all grown up and not a
little tot,
knowing that all those moments was worth
the lot.
But its unconditional there's no turning
back,
we just have do the best with what we
have.
For them our children,
without them our future is lost.
So you see we're all the same,

we all have our box of matches,
to help play the tiresome game.
You see we all want the same,
in this parent game,
and that's the best for little ones,
to grow up,
and not make our mistakes again.

Youth

See now me I don't just talk the truth,
I walk the truth,
I show the youth,
to grow from the knowledge of the past
truth.
In turn they learn to be the past,
and how to last,
never giving up their future hand,
always have a plan,
learnt from the hand that showed them
back in the knowledge land.
You see the future comes down from hand
to hand,
from him to her,
to her to him,
that's how life's learns always have been.
Quick to take quick to steal,
you haven't learnt from the past deal.
So if not learnt in turn,
then your future isn't earnt.
So you will deny,
that talk,
that walk,
that truth to your under youth.
As they need to know,

no fifty cuffs,
no playing ruff.
We need to show them the good stuff.
No gun no violence,
no crime no silence,
no gangs no war.
Your Muma don't need that knock at her door,
someone telling her that her son ain't no more.
As we create them we shape them,
if we don't relate to them,
they just make mistakes then we blame them.
It's not their fault,
it's ours.
So I hope by speaking out it makes them listen,
it makes our children different.
See we need to not be fake,
or they won't follow,
The youth of today,
won't show their youth of tomorrow.

You

When the sun shines up on your face,
I can see you're not of God's mistakes.
He made you strong he made you week,
so that you are so unique.
God made you a lover and a fighter,
so your life would be much brighter.
So make sure you learn from his guidance,
and try to not be so defiant.
Always try and be better than before,
as this life he gives is so to short.
God doesn't want you to waste your time,
on negative things that drain your mind.
You have the strength,
you have the skills,
you just need to believe that you have
the will.
Now God he knows how to teach,
he gives you the tools you just have to
reach.
There's nothing to stop you it's all in your
hands,
see God he has,
all the right plans.
So take this moment in your life,
and show God that he was so right.

He's invested in keeping your life,
and not letting it end before it's right.
See Gods has these plans,
there not always clear,
and not always easy,
so take the time to learn. . . . .
and learn to walk freely. . . . .

Birthday Lady

As one year ends another year starts.
So those close to you are never far apart.
As your family draw near,
to remind you who you are.
That's a the partner to your fella,
and those children dear to your heart.
Now you give love to yours dearly,
as they do to you,
as they know you're so special,
cause of everything you do.
So at this time of year'
and on your special day,
every single one of them,
will show you in their way.
That you mean so much to them,
more than words can say,
And wouldn't want you in their life,
any other way.
They Just want you to know,
your always in their hearts,
Your never far from their thoughts
Because of who you are.
That's a very special kind of lady,
that never falls apart.
That's why they're all with you now,

Baring gifts and cards.
To show their love and support for you,
That one,
That's in their,
Hearts . . . .

Is It Worth It

So I need know,
is it time to let my love for you go.
So I need to know,
can I move on,
on my own.
But then I feel like I'll forget you,
and our love will never been known.
So I ask you to show me,
is it worth me hanging on.
So I ask you to give me,
a sign that it's not wrong.
So I ask you for the last time,
is it worth fighting and carrying on.
You're the only one that can tell me,
is it off or is it on.
Or is it that our love,
has finally sung,
its last song.

You Are The Seasons

For you are every season,
from the breeze to mountain snow,
from the rain drops that fall upon the leaves
of the wild trees that grow.
Now the stars are in your eyes.
And moon is in your soul.
But the sun is your love that blinds me,
and everyone you know.
Given all these things within you not
everyone can see.
The earth and worldly way about you,
is the way that you need to be.
As we are all here right beside you,
feeding off your glee.
So make sure that you take the time to be
at peace with thee.
As the season move so quickly,
that time goes so fast.
So make sure every season that passes,
isn't waisted,
and it lasts.

Thank you for buying my book I do so hope
that you enjoyed it.

I hope you related to it in some way and
that you felt some of what was written.

If you would like to comment on my
writings in any way feel free to email me
your comments @
marchatter.poerty@outlook.com

25656261R00038

Printed in Poland
by Amazon Fulfillment
Poland Sp. z o.o., Wrocław